GUSTAV MAHLER

Adagietto

from Symphony No. 5
aus der Sinfonie Nr. 5

Arranged for Piano by
Bearbeitung für Klavier von

Ian Flint

ALLE RECHTE VORBEHALTEN · ALL RIGHTS RESERVED

EDITION PETERS

LEIPZIG · LONDON · NEW YORK

Editorial Note

The present arrangement attempts to adhere as closely as possible, in all respects, to Mahler's original score. In seeking to realize, in keyboard terms, its characteristic sound-world of string orchestra with harp, a number of compromises have nonetheless been appropriate or inevitable. These fall essentially into two categories:

(1) the reiteration of certain notes (tied in the original) to compensate for the piano's comparative lack of sustaining power, e.g., in bars 5, 21, 22, 42, 49, 69, 70

(2) textural simplification, sometimes involving a redistribution of the original voicing, e.g., in bars 30–31, 58–63, 82–83, 94

Mahler's pizzicato directions and the solo harp part are indicated throughout by staccato dots.

The sustained quality of this piece lends itself particularly well to the 'string' or 'orchestral' sonorities available on an electronic keyboard.

Ian Flint

Note de l'éditeur

Le présent arrangement tente de suivre d'aussi près que possible, à tous égards, la partition originale de Mahler. Dans la transposition au clavier de l'univers sonore d'un orchestre de cordes avec harpe, un certain nombre de compromis se sont néanmoins révélés inévitables, voire souhaitables. Ils se divisent pour l'essentiel en deux catégories :

(1) la répétition de certaines notes (liées dans l'original) pour compenser les sons relativement peu soutenus du piano, par exemple dans les mesures 5, 21, 22, 42, 49, 69, 70

(2) des simplifications de la texture, avec parfois une redistribution des voix, par exemple dans les mesures 30–31, 58–63, 82–83, 94

Les indications de pizzicato de Mahler et la partie de harpe solo sont notées tout du long avec des points de staccato.

La qualité soutenue de cette pièce se prête particulièrement bien aux sonorités de « cordes » ou d'« orchestre » disponibles sur un clavier électronique.

Ian Flint
Traduction : Dennis Collins

Redaktionelle Anmerkung

Das vorliegende Arrangement ist bemüht, sich in jeder Hinsicht so eng wie möglich an Mahlers Vorlage zu halten. Bei der angestrebten Umsetzung ihrer typischen Klangwelt aus Streichorchester mit Harfe für Tasteninstrument waren dennoch einige Kompromisse angebracht oder unvermeidbar. Diese entfallen im wesentlichen auf zwei Kategorien:

(1) die Wiederholung bestimmter (im Original gebundener) Noten, um den beim Klavier relativ rasch verklingenden Ton auszugleichen, z.B. in den Takten 3, 21, 22, 42, 49, 69, 70

(2) strukturelle Vereinfachung, manchmal durch Umverteilen der ursprünglichen Stimmführung, z.B. in den Takten 30–31, 58–63, 82–83, 94

Mahlers Pizzicatoanweisungen und der Solopart für die Harfe sind durchweg mit Staccatopunkten gekennzeichnet.

Die lang ausgehaltenen Klänge dieses Stücks eignen sich besonders gut für die Klangvorgaben »Streicher« oder »Orchester«, die auf elektronischen Tasteninstrumenten zur Verfügung stehen.

Ian Flint
Übersetzung: Anne Steeb/Bernd Müller

Adagietto
(Symphony No. 5)

Gustav Mahler
(1860–1911)

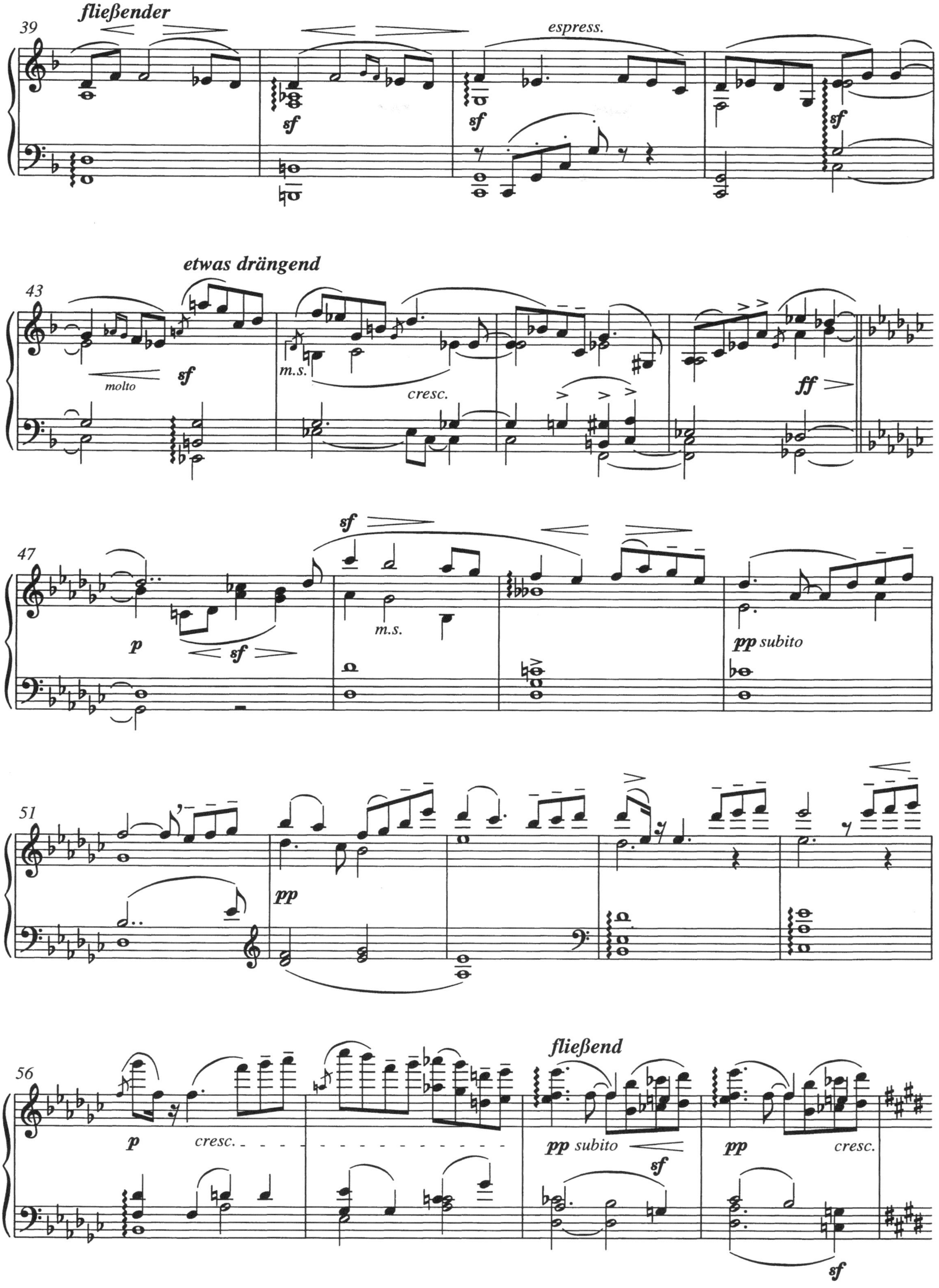

39
fließender
espress.
sf
43
etwas drängend
molto
m.s.
cresc.
ff
47
p
m.s.
pp subito
51
pp
56
fließend
cresc.
pp subito

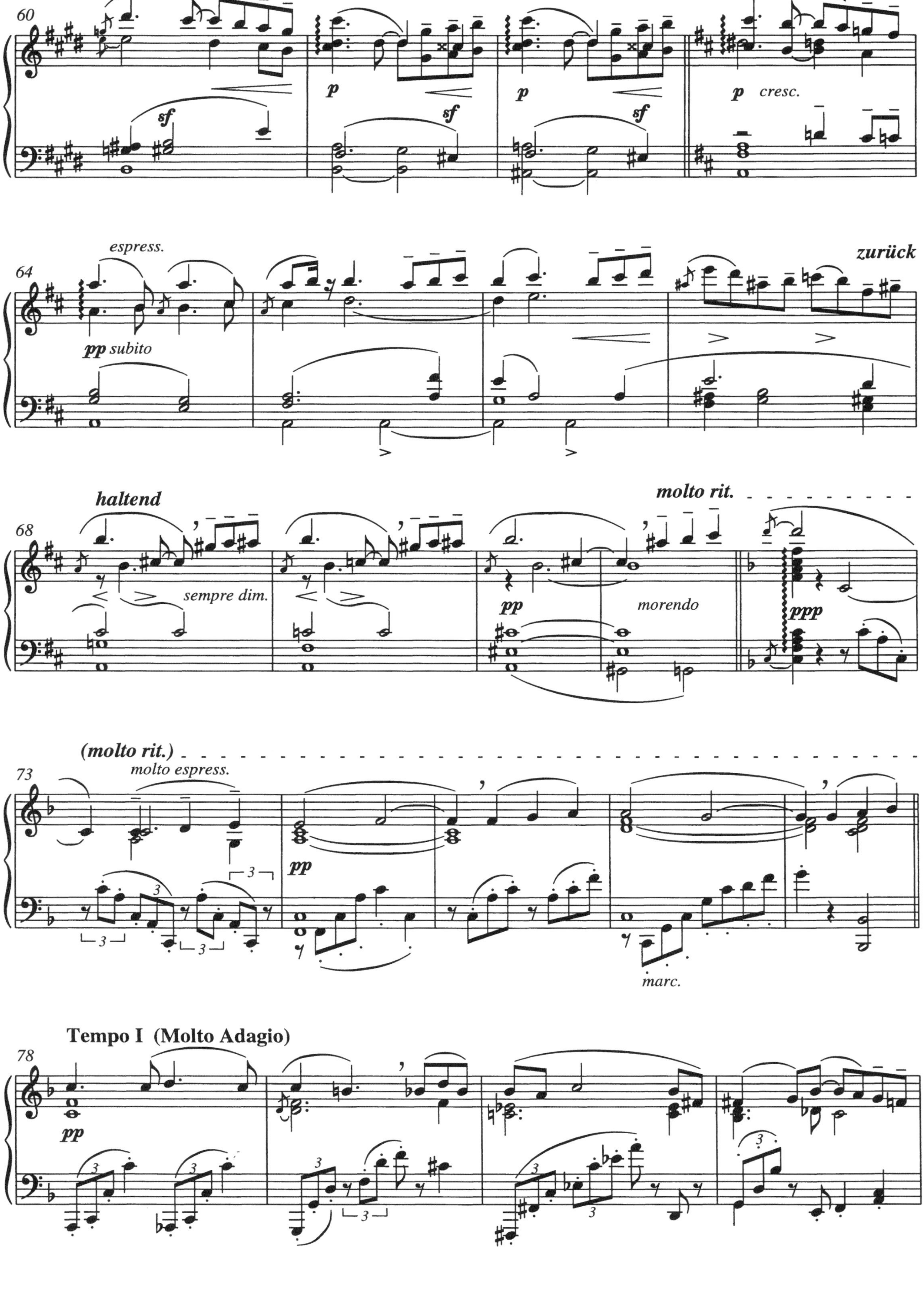
60
p
sf
p
sf
p
sf
p cresc.
64
espress.
pp subito
zurück
68
haltend
sempre dim.
molto rit.
pp
morendo
ppp
73
(molto rit.)
molto espress.
pp
marc.
78
Tempo I (Molto Adagio)
pp